**THIS BOOK IS DEDICATED TO THE CHILDREN OF THE WORLD.
I WILL FOREVER WISH FOR YOUR SAFETY.**

"My Body is Mine" by Crystal Hardstaff
Published by The Gentle Counsellor

2023

Queensland, Australia

www.thegentlecounsellor.com

Second Edition 2024

For any inquiries please contact Crystal Hardstaff at
@thegentlecounsellor or hello@thegentlecounsellor.com

Notes for Parents, Caregivers,

As you know, keeping children safe is a top priority for all of us. One important aspect of child safety is teaching children about body safety. Unfortunately, statistics show that child sexual abuse is all too common. According to the National Sexual Violence Resource Center, 1 in 5 girls and 1 in 20 boys are victims of child sexual abuse. It is therefore crucial that we equip children with the knowledge and tools they need to protect themselves.

Teaching children about body safety can be uncomfortable or difficult for some adults, but it is an essential part of protecting our children. Here are some tips and advice on how to approach this important topic with children:

1. Start early: It is never too early to start teaching children about body safety. Even toddlers can begin learning the proper names for body parts and understanding that some parts of their bodies are private.

2. Use appropriate language: When teaching children about body safety, use age-appropriate language and explanations. Keep it simple and avoid using euphemisms that can be confusing.

3. Reinforce the concept of body autonomy: Help children understand that their bodies belong to them and that they have the right to say "no" to unwanted touches or hugs.

4. Empower children to speak up: Encourage children to speak up if someone tries to touch them inappropriately or makes them feel uncomfortable. Teach them that they have the right to tell a trusted adult and that they will be believed and supported.

5. Teach about safe and unsafe touches: Teach children about the difference between safe and unsafe touches, and help them understand that some touches are only okay with certain people, like a doctor or a parent.

6. Foster open communication: Create an environment of open communication where children feel comfortable talking to you about any concerns or questions they have. Encourage them to come to you with any worries or doubts they may have.

7. Model healthy relationships: Model healthy boundaries and relationships in your own life. Show children what it looks like to respect someone's boundaries and ask for consent.

By teaching children about body safety, we can empower them to protect themselves and prevent abuse. It is up to all of us to keep our children safe and secure.

For any inquiries please contact Crystal Hardstaff at @thegentlecounsellor or hello@thegentlecounsellor.com

This is my body, it's all mine,
And I get to choose, every time,

To run and play, give hugs and high-fives,
And even to speak, to say what's inside!

I take care of my body every day,
Brushing teeth, eating good food, in every way,

Keeping myself clean and wearing clothes,
Taking care of me, that's how it goes.

This is my body, no one can touch it,
Girls have a vulva and vagina as their bits,
Boys have a penis and testicles too,
And we all have bottoms, yes it's true!

Everyone has these parts, you too!
And they may look different, it's nothing new,

But no one has the right to touch or see,
It's private and special for only me.

I love my body, from my head to my toes.
I'm learning to be safe because now I know!

One activity that can be done to explain safe people to a child is using the five fingers of safety as follows:

First, explain the concept of the five fingers of safety to the child, telling them that each finger represents a different aspect of safety. Next, discuss what each finger represents.

For example:

- Thumb: My family and close friends are safe people who I can trust.
- Index finger: People who are safe to be around and who make me feel comfortable.
- Middle finger: People who respect my body and my feelings.
- Ring finger: People who listen to me and take me seriously.
- Pinky finger: People who help keep me safe and protect me.

Have the child go through their own life and identify people who fit into each category. For example, they may put their parents or siblings on the thumb, a favourite teacher on the index finger, a coach or mentor on the middle finger, a grandparent on the ring finger, and a police officer or doctor on the pinky finger.

This activity helps the child understand who safe people are in their lives and helps them learn to identify and seek out safe people in the future.

If someone shows me private parts, that's not ok,
I can say "stop", "no", or "go away",

I'll tell someone I trust what happened that day,
No one can touch me without my say.

There will be times, I need help too,
An adult I trust explains what they're going to do,

Sometimes, when I have to get dressed,
My safe person helps, they're the best!

My Safe People

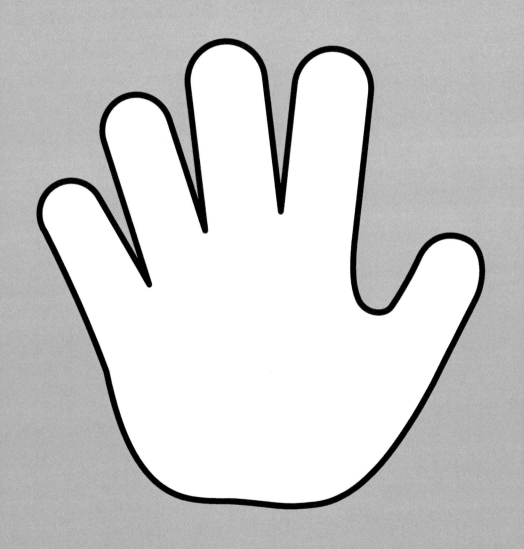

OTHER BOOKS BY
CRYSTAL HARDSTAFF

The 'My Body' Series includes *'My Body is Mine'*, *'My Body, My Choice'*, and *'My Body is Safe'* by Crystal Hardstaff. These books are written for toddlers and young children to be introduced to and help them understand important topics such as the names of their private parts, body safety, consent, tricky people and safe people, and listening to their instincts. This book series was adapted and shortened from the author's original book *'Tricky People'* which covers all these topics and is suitable for young children to school-age.

For more information visit
www.thegentlecounsellor.com

Made in the USA
Las Vegas, NV
18 February 2025

18365631R00019